TACKO FALL
TO NEW HEIGHTS

Tacko Fall & Justin Haynes
illustrated by **Reggie Brown**

CANDLEWICK
ENTERTAINMENT

My name is Tacko Fall. I am seven feet, six inches tall.
Everyone notices me because I am one of the tallest people in the world.

But I have always wanted to be known for more than just my height.

I grew up in Dakar, the capital city of Senegal, in West Africa, with my mom and my younger brother, Fallou. I've always loved playing sports and games. I lived between the beach and the desert, and we played soccer in the rocky sand.

It was hard to find shoes that fit me, and they were expensive, so sometimes I played barefoot. But I always had fun. I learned that what matters isn't how much you have, but what you do with what you have.

I liked school, but I always knew I was different. Although I had many friends, some of my classmates teased me and called me names because I was so tall.

When my classmates' words made me sad, I remembered what my mom told me—that my ancestors were leaders and kings, and that, like them, I should have courage. Her words reminded me that there could be bigger things in my future, that I shouldn't be concerned about small things like teasing and name-calling. There were more important goals to accomplish.

My first real memory of basketball was when we lived at my grandma's house. We only had one TV in the house, and I liked to watch cartoons in the late afternoon. I remember one day my grandma turned off my show so she could watch a basketball game. I was upset at first, but then we watched the game together.

Then when I was twelve, I saw a clip of the famous Dwight Howard Superman dunk. I had never seen someone jump so high. I had no words. I thought Dwight Howard really was a superhero. That was when I became interested in basketball and the NBA.

When one of my friends got a basketball, we started going to the outdoor court not too far from the school just to play around.

It was on that court where my basketball journey really started.

I was discovered by a coaching group, who told me my height was a blessing and that I might find success in this game. They would help me train and condition my body so that I could become a better player. On my first day, I could not run up and down the court without being completely exhausted.

The first time I tried weight lifting, I could not even lift the bar—and there were no weights on it!

There were so many rules
about the game of basketball
that I didn't understand.

But I tried not to let these
things frustrate me, to just
take one step each day.

The more I practiced,
the more I improved.

One day my coach told me I had an opportunity to go to high school in America. In that moment, I began to dream about one day playing in the NBA. The day I left home, I was excited. For a long time, I had wondered what it would be like to get on a plane, go to America, and see the tall buildings. I wanted to see what all the hype was about.

But that excitement turned to sadness as I was leaving the airport in Senegal when I realized that I probably wouldn't see my little brother and my mom for a very long time. But then I remembered what I had learned about having courage. I would need it. It would be seven years before I would see my family again.

I was sixteen years old when I came to America. I did not speak much English, but I knew the basics from school and often tried to engage in conversations with people. TV and music helped a lot. After one month of practice, I was able to converse with my new friends and classmates. After six months, I was fluent.

As my English improved, so did my skills on the basketball court. My hard work led to a scholarship—I was going to play basketball at the University of Central Florida.

Once I got to college, I practiced every day and continued to learn new skills and grow. It was a big campus, so I got around by bike. It was much too small, but it got me where I needed to go.

The more we won, the more people began to notice me. I had become a strong basketball player.

In my senior year, the team reached the second round of the NCAA tournament for the first time. Together we had reached new heights!

After the season, my focus became trying to make it to the NBA.

Even though I had improved a lot, I went undrafted. After the draft, the Celtics were the first team to reach out. I could tell right away that they were willing to help me grow both on and off the court.

I promised that I would practice hard, that I'd have courage, that I wouldn't let anything distract me. I would do whatever it took to be a Boston Celtic and to play in the NBA!

WE WANT

On October 26, 2019, I played in my first NBA game, at Madison Square Garden against the New York Knicks. It was like a movie. Fans from the opposing team rarely cheer for you, but that night, they cheered for me. The energy in the arena was unbelievable. I remember gradually hearing my name from one side of the arena ("We want Tacko!"), and then the whole crowd began to chant it.

Throughout the game, I was very nervous. I was dressed in my jersey, but I didn't know if I was going to play. We started getting a big lead, and then the crowd chanted my name more and more. Finally, Coach told me I was going in the game. I was so nervous, but I tried to stay focused.

After running up and down the court, I started to feel comfortable.
They passed me the ball twice and I missed my first two shots.

On my third chance, I felt like the ball was in my hands forever.

It was only one second, but in that moment my instincts told me to dunk it! Which I did!

The crowd went crazy.

After I scored, I felt so happy that I was living my dream and the fans appreciated me. All the hard work I put in was paying off.

Now I just had to embrace it and keep working.

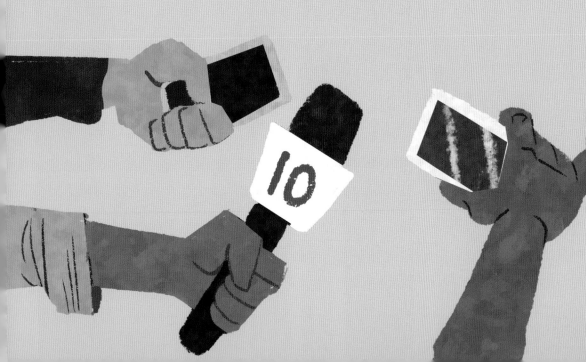

Playing in the NBA has been a dream come true for me, but it wouldn't have happened if I hadn't worked hard, taken risks, and most of all, believed in myself.

Always dream BIG! Always have courage. If you do, you can rise to new heights!

*All my praise to God for all his blessings and for the love
of my mother and my brother. This book is dedicated to you.*

TF

For Laila, Presley, and Noelle, and believing that all your dreams are possible

JH

*To my wonderful friend Mark Lin.
Thank you for always being there and shining a light through the storm.*

RB

First edition 2022

Library of Congress Catalog Card Number pending
ISBN 978-1-5362-1958-6

22 23 24 25 26 27 APS 10 9 8 7 6 5 4 3 2 1

Printed in Humen, Dongguan, China

This book was typeset in Agenda.
The illustrations were created digitally.

Candlewick Entertainment
an imprint of
Candlewick Press
99 Dover Street
Somerville, Massachusetts 02144

www.candlewick.com